SOUTH DEVON MURDER STORIES

A COLLECTION OF MURDER STORIES
FROM AROUND CORNWALL & DEVON

Brendan Hawthorne

BRADWELL
BOOKS

Published by Bradwell Books
11 Orgreave Close Sheffield S13 9NP
Email: books@bradwellbooks.co.uk

British Library Cataloguing in Publication Data: a
catalogue record for this book is available from the
British Library.

1st Edition

ISBN: 9781912060979

Design by: Andy Caffrey

Typesetting: Mark Titterton

Photograph credits: Creative Commons (CC) and Wiki Commons
Print: Gomer Press, Llandysul, Ceredigion SA44 4JL

CONTENTS

INTRODUCTION

FOR A MIDLANDER LIKE ME THE COUNTIES OF DEVON AND CORNWALL HAVE BEEN THE DESTINATION OF MANY HOLIDAYS FROM CHILDHOOD TO MORE RECENT TIMES, A PLACE OF FOND MEMORIES AND BEAUTIFUL LANDSCAPES FROM EYE-WATERING BLISS TO CRASHING ATLANTIC COASTLINES. I HAVE VENTURED AROUND MUCH OF THE COASTLINE, AND MANY PLACES BETWEEN, DRAWING ON THE HISTORY, TRADITIONS AND CULTURES OF EACH LOCALITY I'VE VISITED.

When the opportunity arose for me to research and represent the stories within the covers of this little book, I visited a Devon and Cornwall I'd never been to before. Becoming an archive time traveller allows you not only to see places as they were, but also to step into the minds of the people who lived there and observe the views both visually and culturally of the time.

The landscape holds many stories, and crime through the ages is never far away from law and order. The old trade routes by sea, river and land brought wealth, but also demise and murder. One person's wealth is another person's desire. One person's desire is another's jealousy and, whether that wealth be coin or love, they are powerful emotions. When these emotions are set

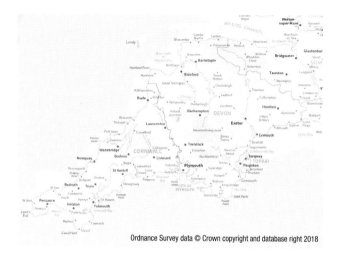

Ordnance Survey data © Crown copyright and database right 2018

against poverty and greed the atmosphere becomes a complex and heady blend of intrigue.

Whether a local or a visitor to the region, this book gives the reader a brief insight into some of the historical murders in the locale. If you are searching for concise reading when travelling or relaxing or, indeed, seeking further references to stories beyond this book, this publication is for you.

Insatiable Murderous Greed

AS THE NOOSE TIGHTENED AROUND THOMAS AUSTIN'S NECK AT EXETER JAIL IN AUGUST OF 1694 ONE WONDERS WHETHER ANY REMORSE WAS FELT AT HIS TRANSITION FROM LIFE TO DEATH. ONE THING WAS CERTAIN. NINE PEOPLE LAY SLAIN BY AUSTIN'S HAND, AND ALL IN THE NAME OF MONEY.

The small community of late-seventeenth-century Cullompton went about its rural idyllic business as usual. Class division would have been evident, but both landowners and labourers used the busy route through

Cullompton Martin Bodman CC

mid Devon, which brought work and workers to and from the farmsteads. However, in 1694 tranquil beauty was replaced with the screams of innocent people as they were cut down, one by one, at the hands of a wealthy man, born into money and born to let it slip through his bloodstained fingers.

Thomas Austin was the son of a family of self-made prosperity and his parents are described as 'hardworking'. Upon their deaths, all of the family wealth went into the coffers of their son. The businesses the Austins had built up over the years supplied a healthy annual return and should have provided Thomas Austin with a lifestyle to be envied. He was seen by many other wealthy farming families as someone their daughters should marry. Eventually, Thomas married the daughter of a nearby farmer who supplied as a dowry an amount that was a small fortune at the time. But unfortunately for Thomas Austin, his bride and his victims, he did not have the acumen to keep his inherited wealth intact and soon bad decisions, costs and a profligate lifestyle were outweighing his income, leading him to take desperate measures.

It began with a failed attempt to rework his land, followed by borrowing money from friends and neighbours, who bailed him out without return. Eventually, the demands of a spent-out reputation left Austin effectively bankrupt.

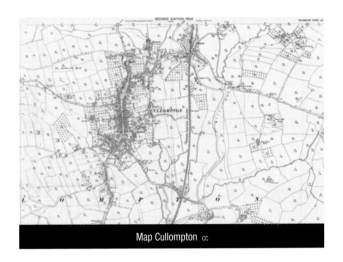

Map Cullompton cc

Austin needed money – lots of it – to pay for his excesses and, in an act of desperation, was no longer going to ask for charity. He was going to do what it took to get back on an even footing, whatever the cost.

Highway robbery offered rich pickings along the routes to market towns. A great deal of money was carried about the person and Austin knew this. His life of crime had begun, holding up the unsuspecting traveller to hand over their riches. On one occasion the handover of wealth resulted in a confrontation.

Sir Zachary Wilmott always travelled with cash. The locals knew this and, therefore, so did Austin. This particular day, Austin attempted to lighten Sir Zachary's load by robbing him of 46 guineas and a silver-hilted sword. Wilmott fought back and, drawing a pistol, Austin became a murderer in the flash of a flintlock pan.

The murder caused an outrage, but Austin escaped notice or suspicion through the honour of his family's frayed but still respected standing. Remaining silent and unquestioning, Austin's wife continued to raise their two children in what was becoming a pressured relationship. Every time there was a knock on the door, another call was made for payments and soon the ill-gotten gains were spent.

It appears Austin had a choice: return to robbery or go to his uncle and explain his dire situation. He would need to throw himself on his uncle's financial mercy. Austin travelled the mile to his uncle's residence, only to find him out on business. His family asked him to wait, but Austin snapped and took a hatchet to the head of his aunt. As her five children ran, he picked up a knife from the kitchen and systematically slit the throats of the innocents before ransacking the house for £60, which was about three quarters of his inherited annual income.

On his arrival back home, Austin's wife questioned his bloodstained clothes, sending Austin into another rage, in which he cut his wife's throat and mutilated his own two children, the eldest just three years of age. At that moment, Austin's uncle paid him a visit to see what help his nephew needed, only to be greeted with a horrific scene of carnage. Austin boasted about what his uncle would find on his return. Straight away, his uncle went home to see what his nephew had done and immediately returned, knocking Austin unconscious and arranging for his arrest, which would ultimately lead to his trial and execution. The people said that Austin had it coming, that he had fully deserved the executioner's ordered drop for what he had done, all in the name of money.

Exeter Prison   Thos Austin CC

Death of a Dymond at Rough Tor

A CHILL WIND BLOWS ACROSS BODMIN MOOR EVEN ON THE WARMEST OF DAYS, ITS REMOTE CHARM DRAWING IN VISITORS FROM AROUND THE WORLD. ONE VISITOR, THOUGH, DRESSED IN HER SUNDAY BEST CLOTHING, IS NOW THE RESTLESS SPIRIT OF CHARLOTTE DYMOND, MURDERED IN THE NAME OF LOVE AND LEFT TO WANDER ROUGH TOR SINCE 1844.

Rough Tor is Cornwall's second highest peak, but in April 1844 it became better known as the scene of murderous intent, or so the records would have it. Lying in a ditch over a week after her sudden disappearance and the rumour of her being offered a job at Blisland, the body of Charlotte Dymond was found. She still wore her green Sunday dress and a red shawl about her person. Her throat had been cut with force and her body put into a ditch near to the River Allen to hide the horror of such a death on this route from Camelford to Davidstow.

Charlotte Dymond was of illegitimate birth and flirtatious by nature, as well as being reportedly easy on the eye. She had attracted two suitors from her work as a domestic servant at Penhale Farm. The farm was owned by a widow and her son, who employed Charlotte and two farm hands, Matthew Weekes and John Stevens, who were both in their twenties. Matthew Weekes was said to not be the best-looking of men and it was a surprise to many that he and Charlotte and Matthew may have become an 'item'. Matthew was said to have few teeth, was short in stature and carried a pronounced limp. However, he was not alone in his intentions towards Charlotte. Farm labourer Thomas Prout, the well-dressed nephew of the farm owner, was overheard by John Stevens boasting that he could take Charlotte from Matthew and, indeed, it was found out later that Charlotte and Thomas had planned to elope.

On Sunday 14 April 1844, Charlotte and Matthew were seen walking on the moors. A witness recognised him by his gait that day and when Matthew returned to the farm alone that evening, his clothes muddied and bloodied, his shirt collar torn, suspicion was raised.

The story of the Blisland position a few miles away, which might have explained the disappearance of Charlotte, was checked out by John Stevens. The story was untrue and now Matthew Weekes also could not be found. Circumstantial evidence led to Weekes being named as the murderer. The search for him ended in Plymouth. Weekes had been found at his sister's house planning his escape to the Channel Islands and in possession of a blood-spotted ladies' handkerchief and a pair of ladies' gloves. However circumstantial the evidence was, Weekes was arrested and tried for murder on 2 August.

Pleading his innocence, he suggested that Charlotte's death had been a matter of suicide, as it was rumoured she was pregnant. After a brief half hour in court, Weekes was found guilty and taken to Bodmin Jail, spending ten days there awaiting execution. It is said he was the author of two letters, though both are written in language beyond the literacy of one so poorly educated. One letter of moral guidance read:

> *'I hope young men will take a warning by me and not put too much confidence in young women, the same as I did; and I hope young females will take the same by young men. I loved that girl as dear as I loved my life; and after all the kind treatment I have showed her, and then she said she would have nothing more to do with me. And after this was done, then bitterly I did lament, thinking what would be my end. And I thank the judge and jury too, for they have given me no more than was my due.'*

There is some evidence that suggests that court scribes would write such letters in cases of admission of guilt in order to hold unfortunates like this as an example to others. At noon on 12 August Matthew Weekes

Stannon Stone circle   Chris Andrews CC

was finally hanged in front of several thousand people gathered at Bodmin Jail. His body was later buried in the coal yard.

There was no doubt that Charlotte had been brutally murdered. That Weekes was indeed the guilty party was not in doubt among the local community, who subscribed to a monument in memory of Charlotte that read:

'This monument is erected by public subscription in memory of Charlotte Dymond who was murdered here by Matthew Weekes on Sunday April 14 1844'

THIS
MONUMENT
is ERECTED by
PUBLIC
SUBSCRIPTION
in
MEMORY
of
CHARLOTTE DYMOND
who was MURDERED here
by
MATTHEW WEEKES
on
SUNDAY
April 14
1844

Charlotte Dymond Monument Roger Marks CC

This crime of passion led poet Charles Causley to write the following:

The Ballad of Charlotte Dymond

It was a Sunday evening
And in the April rain
That Charlotte went from our house
And never came home again.

Her shawl of diamond redcloth,
She wore a yellow gown,
She carried the green gauze handkerchief
She bought in Bodmin town.

About her throat her necklace
And in her purse her pay:
The four silver shillings
She had at Lady Day.

In her purse four shillings
And in her purse her pride
As she walked out one evening
Her lover at her side.

Out beyond the marshes
Where the cattle stand,
With her crippled lover
Limping at her hand.

Charlotte walked with Matthew
Through the Sunday mist,
Never saw the razor
Waiting at his wrist.

Charlotte she was gentle
But they found her in the flood
Her Sunday beads among the reeds
Beaming with her blood.

Matthew, where is Charlotte,
And wherefore has she flown?
For you walked out together
And now are come alone.

Why do you not answer,
Stand silent as a tree,
Your Sunday worsted stockings
All muddied to the knee?

Why do you mend your breast-pleat
With a rusty needle's thread
And fall with fears and silent tears
Upon your single bed?

Why do you sit so sadly
Your face the colour of clay
And with a green gauze handkerchief
Wipe the sour sweat away?

Has she gone to Blisland
To seek an easier place,
And is that why your eye won't dry
And blinds your bleaching face?

South West MURDERS

Take me home! cried Charlotte,
'I lie here in the pit!
A red rock rests upon my breasts
And my naked neck is split!'

Her skin was soft as sable,
Her eyes were wide as day,
Her hair was blacker than the bog
That licked her life away;

Her cheeks were made out of honey,
Her throat was made of flame
Where all around the razor
Had written its red name.

As Matthew turned at Plymouth
About the tilting Hoe,
The cold and cunning constable
Up to him did go:

'I've come to take you, Matthew,
Unto the magistrate's door.
Come quiet now, you pretty poor boy,
And you must know what for.'

'She is as pure,' cried Matthew,
'As is the early dew,
Her only stain it is the pain
That round her neck I drew!

'She is as guiltless as the day
She sprang forth from her mother.
The only sin upon her skin
Is that she loved another.'

They took him off to Bodmin,
They pulled the prison bell,
They sent him smartly up to heaven
And dropped him down to hell.

All through the granite kingdom
And on its travelling airs
Ask which of these two lovers
The most deserves your prayers.

And your steel heart search, Stranger,
That you may pause and pray
For lovers who come not to bed
Upon their wedding day,

But lie upon the moorland
Where stands the sacred snow
Above the breathing river,
And the salt sea-winds go.

Author's Great Grandfather's Murder & a Fearful Premonition

A WADEBRIDGE ENTREPRENEUR IS BRUTALLY SET UPON WHEN RETURNING HOME FROM BODMIN MARKET. UPON HIS PERSON HE CARRIED A FULL PURSE, WHICH WAS SEEN BY THE OPPORTUNIST LIGHTFOOT BROTHERS, AND ON A LONELY, DESOLATE AND WOODED ROAD THEY STALKED THEIR PREY AS HE RODE ALONE AND DELIVERED THE DEADLY CONSEQUENCES.

Camel Wadebridge   Derek Harper CC

The morning of 8 February 1840 started with the usual ten-mile horseback journey from Wadebridge to the regular market day in Bodmin. Nevell Norway saddled his small grey mare and rode through the Pencarrow Estate to go about his business. His main work as a timber importer and shipping merchant afforded him a philanthropic lifestyle and brought him much respect in his community.

Born in 1801, Nevell was raised in Egloshayle, having eight other siblings. His family were generationally known as traders and were well liked in the area. On that fateful day, Nevell had emptied his purse of gold and silver coins into the palm of his hand to buy some goods from a fellow trader.

Nevell Norway CC

The Lightfoot brothers, William and James (also from Egloshayle), were drawn to the treasure that lay before them and hatched their plan to accost Nevell on his way home and relieve him of his finances.

However, Nevell didn't go straight home once the market had closed for the day. Instead, he stayed in Bodmin until 10 pm, when he and his acquaintance Mr Hambly decided to ride in the direction of Wadebridge together. This they did for a third of the journey until

Mr Hambly turned off the road to continue to his own destination, leaving Nevell to ride past the wooded areas that lay between him and home.

Nevell's brother Edmund was Chief Officer aboard the ship *Orient* and was at that very moment recording in the ship's log an horrific dream he had had at 9.45 that evening. He saw two men attack his brother with a pistol. He described the brutal attack in great detail, even down to the exact point on the road, including changes to the road that had happened since he had sailed, but wouldn't know of the accuracy of his dream for a further six months on his return to Britain.

Later that night, a riderless grey horse was stopped and recognised by locals walking home. A search led to the discovery of the body of Nevell lying in a stream at Northill. He was pronounced dead by Dr Tickell. Further examination recorded the cause of death as repeated blows to the head, administered with a blunt object. There were powder marks beneath the chin, too, revealing a gunshot wound to the head.

The crime scene also revealed that a struggle had taken place and that the body had been dragged to the point at which it was found, the assailants leaving two sets of distinctive footprints behind a hedge where they had nervously lain in wait to commit their robbery most foul. A broken pistol lock lay not far from the pool of blood that still stained the earth.

A reward of £100 led to very little information coming forward, although it was reported that the Lightfoots had been seen near to Nevell's empty house that night. A blacksmith neighbour of James Lightfoot heard him and his wife arguing through the partition of their properties. James Lightfoot tried to calm and quieten down his wife and child, but his wife wouldn't be silent. Six days later a pistol missing its lock was found by police hidden in a ceiling beam at the home of James Lightfoot. Keys to Nevell's house were also found, presumably stolen by the Lightfoots to take more from their dead victim while they could.

James Lightfoot cc

James Lightfoot's guilt was evident and further witness statements implicated both brothers. On 17 February the Lightfoot brothers were arrested and formally charged with the murder and robbery of Nevell Norway, and they met their fate at Cornwall's Lent Assizes. On 30 March they were found guilty of murder and after seeing their families for the last time were hanged at Bodmin Jail on 13 April. Reports from the time suggested a crowd in excess of 10,000 spectators gathering to observe the hanging, the numbers augmented by special trains being laid on to ferry people into Bodmin.

Nevell Norway was buried in the churchyard at Egloshayle where a monument was erected to his memory. His wife and six children were left in poverty, though local subscriptions raised a substantial sum to support them. Nevell Norway was the great grandfather of the novelist Nevil Shute, author of *On the Beach* and *A Town Like Alice*.

Solicitor Found Guilty of Murder!

PLYMOUTH-BORN MAJOR HERBERT ROWSE ARMSTRONG, WHO SERVED IN WORLD WAR I WITH THE ROYAL ENGINEERS AND WAS DECORATED FOR LONG SERVICE, BECAME A CORNERSTONE OF HIS COMMUNITY AND PROFESSION IN THE POST-WAR YEARS. HOWEVER, FROM BATTLEFIELD TO HOME, HIS CONFLICTS AND CONQUESTS CONTINUED AND AS PERSONAL AFFAIRS FLARED UP THE ONLY OUTCOME WAS A DEADLY ONE.

Major Herbert Rowse Armstrong cc

On 31 May 1922, Herbert Rowse Armstrong swung from the end of a rope at Gloucester Prison, the only solicitor ever to hang for murder. He was a father of three, a Freemason and held in high regard within the communities he served. But behind the doors of this well-regarded man lay dark motives leading to murderous intentions.

His life had been fairly nomadic. Born on 13 May 1869, Herbert made his way through the halls of academia from a modest upbringing, graduating through St Catharine's College, Cambridge. He became a solicitor and moved to Liverpool and then to Newton Abbot, before settling down with his Devon-born wife, affectionately known as Kitty, in Hay-on-Wye.

Upon returning from active service during the last six months of the war, Rowse Armstrong noted that Kitty had begun to suffer from both mental and physical disorders. She was finally admitted to Barnwood, a private mental hospital in Gloucester, suffering from various physical problems diagnosed by her medic Dr Hincks. These included a heart murmur, chest and kidney problems and partial paralysis. Major Armstrong kept in close contact with Dr Hincks, as any concerned husband would, but what were his motives for such close contact?

In January of 1921, Kitty returned home with much-improved health, her doting husband sitting with her each evening, but within a month Dr Hincks was writing the cause of her demise as gastritis on her death certificate. Some say Kitty had been a nasty character, always ridiculing her husband in public; others say Armstrong's roving eye for the ladies contributed to domestic pressures. It is reported that the Armstrongs' servants drew the curtains as a mark of respect to the death of Kitty. On his return home, Major Armstrong opened them.

Major Armstrong, it seems, had a dislike of dandelions, even when out of season, and regularly bought small amounts of arsenic from the local chemist's run by John Davies, the father-in-law of Oswald Martin, to rid his garden of the invasive weed. Oswald Martin was the only competitor in Hay for legal services. Both Major Armstrong and Oswald Martin had become embroiled in a legal battle over a land sale, resulting in Oswald Martin being due to receive a substantial sum of money from the Major's client. However, it is alleged that Major Armstrong had already spent the money made available by his client and, therefore needed to stall the completion and to literally 'buy' time. The only way the Major could do this was to knock Oswald Martin out of competition for a while.

A box of chocolates was anonymously sent to the Martin household. Oswald Martin's sister succumbed to temptation and soon fell ill, leaving the rest of the chocolates untouched. Following this incident, the Major then invited Martin to his home for afternoon tea and a chat. The Major passed a scone to Martin by hand, saying 'Excuse fingers', which seemed strange. When Martin returned home he was violently ill, symptoms

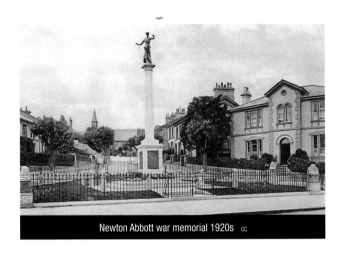

Newton Abbott war memorial 1920s cc

which Dr Hincks had seen before. John Davies advised Martin against receiving any further gratuities from the Major, as suspicions began to rise about Armstrong's purchasing and use of arsenic.

The doctor, fearing the worst, asked to see the chocolates that had been left untouched by Martin's sister. They were each found to have a small hole in the base into which arsenic had been placed. Dr Hincks' examination of Martin's urine revealed traces of arsenic. The findings were passed on to the Home Office and, eventually, Scotland Yard. In the meantime, the Major's further invitations to tea were met with Martin's repeated refusal to return. The Major was finally arrested on suspicion of murder. A small pouch of white powder was found upon his person. The powder was arsenic.

On 3 April 1922, the trial of Major Rowse Armstrong began. Reports of Kitty taking her own life were quickly dismissed. It was revealed that Kitty had left her estate to the children and not to the Major. However, the Major produced a new will, supposedly written by his late wife, giving him full control of her estate. It was revealed that Kitty's estate would not have covered the shortfall in her husband's debts and although the Major hung his innocence on circumstantial evidence, the jury thought that the only outcome was one of a guilty verdict. Just before the trapdoor opened on the Major, he called out, 'Kitty I'm coomin' to ye!'

A Bridge Too Far

THE SMALL DEVON VILLAGE OF PETER TAVY LIES THREE MILES NORTH-EAST OF THE TOWN OF TAVISTOCK. ON A DARK AND TORMENTED NIGHT IN NOVEMBER 1893 IT WAS SUBJECT TO A HORRIFIC SCENE. YOUTHFUL SCREAMS OF PLAYFUL LAUGHTER TURNED TO TEARS AND CRIES OF HORROR AS A VULNERABLE YOUNG MAN COULD CONTAIN HIS ANGER NO MORE.

The village of Peter Tavy is built upon granite and is situated in the moorlands of Devon. It is known for its farming traditions, both dairy and agricultural, and its predictable patterns of life give a sense of idyllic calm. It was always seen as a good place to grow up, with all the freedoms and trusts that are found in an area that had seen little in the way of recorded violence.

At eighteen years of age, William Williams was a known epileptic and was academically challenged. He was regarded as being a little 'slow on the uptake' and was unfortunately tormented by his late teenaged and twenty-something peers. Everyone knew William, but it appears that they didn't know the full extent of his mental incapacity. He had a family history of relatives with mental health problems and that may have been the reason for his subsequent violent actions.

William had fallen deeply in love with seventeen-year-old Emma Doidge. His love, it appears, went mainly unrequited, or, at least was not taken too seriously. On the Sunday of 17 November Emma was unwittingly going to meet her fate on an evening that was, to all intents and purposes, just like any other Sunday night. Emma sang at the local church with her sister Elizabeth and a group of fellow friends and choristers. After their evening choir practice, the group were met by Emma's brother (confusingly also named William). Stopping to chat, the group waited as they all gathered outside into small huddles for private conversations. Organ blower William Rowe, who was also seeking the affections of Emma Doidge, stood nearby hoping to gain the attentions of Emma whilst the socialising continued.

Suddenly, William Williams, who had joined in with the group, began an argument with Emma. Emma's brother heard the angry young man swearing at his sister and so promptly stepped in to avoid further upset. Williams squared up to Emma's brother, offering to fight out their differences. William Williams then threatened to 'knock Emma's head off'. On hearing this, Emma's brother continued in his attempt to calm things down, saying that the threat wouldn't be carried out while he was there. William Williams had the last word, though, shouting to Emma's brother, 'I have finished with you, Bill, but someone will be floored tonight.' William Williams walked off ahead of the group towards

Longford, possibly hearing the jeers from the crowd and cruel comments on his admission of his devoted love for Emma.

Emma's brother had different ideas on how the evening was going, as he had romantic leanings toward a Miss Mudge, who was also party to the argument. The group offered to walk Emma and her sister home, but Emma elected to walk home with her true love, William Rowe. Chillingly, as the group left the pair to their short walk home, they suddenly heard gunshots ring out.

Elizabeth Doidge ran towards her father's home fearing the worst. This was realised when Mr Doidge quickly discovered the body of the slain Rowe and a few paces on he found his daughter with an open head wound that was sickeningly pouring away her life. As the story unfolded, it became apparent that Williams had indeed shot the couple and then attempted suicide. The suicide attempt, however, took on some farcical elements, Williams scraping only the brim of his hat with his first attempt. Williams then shot himself through the right eye, which only served to blind him in that eye. The bullet lodged in his brain and was later retrieved by a doctor. In a crazed state, he stumbled his way to a nearby bridge and hurled himself into the stream. Unfortunately, for his intentions, the water was only a foot or so deep and so he managed to stand up quite easily. Full of remorse and with a bloody face and muddied body, he staggered

Bridge at Peter Tavy Tony Atkin CC

Church Peter Tavy Tony Atkin CC

to a nearby house where he was given a drink and his father was called for. On his father's arrival, Williams confessed to both shootings and only showed remorse for killing twenty-one-year-old Frederick Rowe. Williams also confessed that it wasn't the taunts that had driven him to this awful deed, but that Emma had not acknowledged his letters. Almost matter of factly, he told his father that he had made Emma beg for her life. He didn't listen to her plea and revengefully pulled the trigger on her.

At the trial, Williams' own father became chief witness and, interestingly, none of the accused's mental conditions were reported until it was too late for them to be used as admissible grounds for mental incapacity.

The judge in his summing up dubbed it the 'worst crime ever' and on 28 March 1893, at the age of nineteen, William Williams faced the noose at Exeter. His body was later removed and buried in the grounds of the prison under a layer of quicklime, which was often used to accelerate the decomposition of the body as it lay in the ground. Some may wonder whether this was a final act of judicial vengeance for a crime so foul, or did it save Williams' mortal remains from further unwanted interest?

Titanic Battle to Prove Innocence

WE HEAR MANY STORIES OF THOSE POOR UNFORTUNATES LOST ON THAT FATEFUL NIGHT OF 15 APRIL 1912 IN THE NORTH ATLANTIC ABOARD THE WHITE STAR LINER *TITANIC*. MANY NAMES CAME TO THE FORE FOR THEIR ACTS OF BRAVERY, OTHERS FOR ALLEGED ACTS OF CORPORATE MANSLAUGHTER AND OTHERS FOR INCOMPETENCE OR COWARDICE THAT LED TO 'UNNECESSARY' DEATH AND SUFFERING. CORNISHMAN ROBERT HICHENS, ONE OF SIX QUARTERMASTERS, OR HELMSMEN, ABOARD THE VESSEL, FOUND HIMSELF CHARGED OF THE LATTER.

Born on 16 September 1882 in Newlyn, Cornwall, you could say that Robert Hichens' life was literally 'all at sea.' He had been a sailor since the age of fourteen and by the time he was thirty years of age had become a quartermaster on board the *Titanic*. He was regarded as a loyal and caring man with a good sense of humour, but his life would be defined by his actions aboard Lifeboat 6 as the *Titanic* slipped into the icy waters of the North Atlantic, the order of 'hard a starboard' still sounding in his head.

Robert Hitchens cc

On the evening of 14 April 1912, Hichens took orders to steer the ship away from an iceberg that had loomed out of the darkness and was on a collision course with the liner. The iceberg was only seen at the last minute, as the calm sea had cut no waves on the shores of the berg. Hichens either misheard or misunderstood the order and was later accused of steering the ship towards the jagged ice instead of away from it.

Aboard Lifeboat 6 he successfully navigated the vessel away from the suction of the *Titanic* as it went down, saving the lives of forty people. Again he was criticised for not returning to people who were still in the icy water calling out for their lives. There were several lifeboats positioned in 'safe' waters, but one of Hichens' passengers, influential American socialite Mrs Molly Brown, made her views and feelings very well known. A statement issued Stateside accused Hichens of saying that it was pointless going back to the site of the stricken vessel as the passengers in the water were already 'stiffs'. This word to describe the doomed passengers could perhaps be considered a turn of phrase that a Cornishman would not use.

Following two enquiries into the sinking of the liner without charge, the Hichens family moved to Torquay, but the pressures of the disaster and subsequent news reports that followed only fuelled the labels of 'cowardice' and of 'being a bully', which caused the family to split up. Hichens remained in Torquay, making two suicide attempts and beginning to drink heavily. His wife and children had no choice in separating from this changed man and moved to Southampton, leaving the beleaguered figure of Hichens to face his demons.

Needing to get his life back to something he could control and, therefore, overcome his nervous disorder (today this would be considered post-traumatic stress disorder) Hichens set up his own company. He bought boats and chartered them out. This may have been seen as 'therapy' in hindsight, but the pressures of business must have contributed to latent emotions surfacing once more, which ultimately led Hichens to buy a gun. Whether the purpose of this purchase was to use it on himself is unclear, but one thing he did do was to shoot one of his business associates, Harry Henley. Henley had sold Hichens a boat, which had led to an altercation with Henley over some financial issues. As Henley survived the incident, Hichens was jailed for the assault and went on to serve a four-year jail term, and was finally released from physical incarceration in 1937.

Over the next three years, the sad figure of Hichens attempted to put the pieces of his shattered life back together, but the rumours, taunts and horrors of 2340 hours on 14 April 1912 haunted both Hichens personally and in his subsequent working life. He managed to find some work on a cargo ship during the Second World

War as third mate, delivering goods around the world. His last voyage delivered coal to Africa and returned to Scotland. As the vessel *English Trader* docked on 23 September 1940 at Aberdeen, a crew member went to wake Hichens from his slumbers as he lay in his bunk. Hichens never awoke from that sleep and, it appears, he had died of heart failure. He was 59.

A man who loved the sea and his family, who became the target for the outpouring of emotions following the tragic deaths of those aboard the *Titanic*, and who later faced investigations on both sides of the Atlantic was never to return to his homeland of Cornwall. He had passed away a broken man in his fifties. Hichens' granddaughter believes from her research that he died of 'a broken heart'. Hichens, 'the man who sank the *Titanic*', was buried at Trinity Cemetery in Aberdeen, where one would hope he could finally rest in peace.

Beyond the Boundary – Last Man at Bristol Jail

SEEMINGLY ALWAYS A TROUBLED PERSON, MILES WILLIAM GIFFARD WAS BORN IN 1925. HE LIVED HIS ACADEMIC LIFE AT RUGBY SCHOOL IN WARWICKSHIRE AND BLUNDELL'S SCHOOL, TIVERTON. HE WENT ON TO PLAY CRICKET FOR CORNWALL BEFORE BEING HANGED AT THE END OF A NOOSE ON 24 FEBRUARY 1953 AT BRISTOL'S HORFIELD PRISON FOR A DOUBLE MURDER. HE WAS AGED JUST 27.

'An idle little waster' were the damning words of a doctor when summing up the nature of the then twenty-six year-old Miles Giffard. Psychiatric reports had started twelve years earlier to discover the true nature of this young and promising sportsman, yet still he was left with a deteriorating mental condition that would lead to brutal and murderous consequences on 7 November 1952.

Charles and Elizabeth Giffard were well respected and were pillars of the community in St Austell where they lived. Charles was a solicitor and Clerk of the Court in the town and Elizabeth was involved with local Conservatism through the local Conservative Women's Association where she held the position of President. Some reports suggest, however, that the overbearing nature of Miles's parents, especially his father, led to a toxic relationship. Miles, it was thought, lived off his parents as a form of vindictive payback for the strict rules that his parents laid down for him. His mindset had already switched to that of a revenge-driven personality awaiting a final dramatic deed.

Miles had served time in the Navy and then found that he couldn't hold down a day job for any length of time on Civvy Street. It appeared that Miles had found his sporting vocation as a cricketer and in 1948, at 23 years old, Miles William Giffard played cricket for his home county of Cornwall, as well as Minor Counties teams. He played at Kennington Oval with Surrey's Second XI and for Cornwall against Devon at Penzance in that defining sporting year.

Unfortunately, the dark side of Miles's personality was about to resurface and his moody manner and his desire to fuel those fears with drink took over once more. Within his reports of mental instabilities schizophrenia was apparent but largely, it appears, went unchecked. Miles had periods of getting his life back on track, one of which materialised in meeting nineteen-year-old Gabrielle Vallance. Gabrielle lived in London and through Giffard's infatuation with her a serious relationship began. However, Charles and Elizabeth were both displeased with the ensuing relationship and made their feelings known. On hearing their views, Miles spiralled deeper into depression. His parents' displeasure eventually boiled over in a letter from Miles to Gabrielle where he reportedly told her that he could see no future while his father was alive.

On 7 November Miles Giffard started drinking at home. This, it seems, was a direct consequence of his parents telling him to put a halt to the meaningful relationship he had developed with Gabrielle. Miles had earlier in the day asked his father if he could borrow the family car. His father refused, before he and Elizabeth left the house for the afternoon taking the car and leaving Miles at home with his demons. Increasingly, the desire to kill his parents manifested into a course of action that would lead to both his parents being beaten to death with a length of lead pipe upon their return home that evening.

As his father put the car into the garage, Miles lay in wait for the opportunity to strike out and began raining down blows on his father's head. Thinking he had done him in, he went into the kitchen where his mother was served in the same way. Bloodstained Miles went out to where his father lay, only to find him still alive. He calmly placed his father's body into a wheelbarrow and disposed of the body at the end of the family garden, which backed onto a cliff edge. He then went back into the kitchen to find his mother still clinging to life. The wheelbarrow was used again in delivering the body over the edge. In a state of drunkenness, Miles phoned Gabrielle to say that his father had changed his mind and that he could use the car after all. He then drove to see his beloved in London.

Next day, the badly beaten bodies of Charles and Elizabeth Giffard were found at the foot of the cliff by police. An immediate manhunt for Miles was launched. It took little time to find and arrest him for the double murder of his parents. Bloodstained clothes were found in the vehicle that had been at the root of this tragic and brutal turn of events.

The Times newspaper reported on the trial that took place on 5 February 1953, announcing 'Murder Charge Against Son, Evidence Of Grave Mental Disorder'. By 25 February, the same newspaper was announcing the final outcome of the trial: 'Giffard Executed'. The jury had taken a little over half an hour to decide on the fate of Miles Giffard. His history of mental incapacities, no matter how well documented, could not save him from the rope at a Bristol Jail.

Easels and Stones

WOULD NO ONE SUPPLY A COFFIN FOR JOHN WARE? AFTER SERVING A TWELVE-MONTH JAIL SENTENCE FOR ASSAULTING A WOMAN, WARE RETURNED TO THE PLACE HE KNEW BEST. THE TOWN OF HATHERLEIGH IS SITUATED CLOSE TO OKEHAMPTON AND THE

River Lew below Hatherleigh
Derek Harper CC

STRAWBRIDGE AREA OF THE RIVER LEW. BUT HIS FREEDOM WAS TO BE SHORT-LIVED.

News spread quickly about a brutal murder that had taken place near to the town. Soon Ware's past caught up with him and he was lined up as chief suspect in the murder inquiry. He was subsequently arrested and questioned before being left in the cells while police officers reinvestigated a potential crime scene based on new evidence. Upon their return to the cells, the body of John Ware lay lifeless on the floor, having banged his head from a fall caused by self-strangulation. Blood had leaked from his ears, such was the impact.

A scarf had been drawn tightly about his neck, causing unconsciousness and death. No one, though, would supply a coffin for his mortal remains as the story unfolded that he had brutally murdered thirty-three-year-old Mary Breton while she painted the idyllic scenery that had brought so much to her artistic life.

Mary, a visiting artist to Hatherleigh, found peace and inspiration in her surroundings when spending time with her uncle there. She was known and liked by the locals and always had time for a chat. May of 1905 was to shatter that peace with a horrific murder whose silent witnesses lay in a collection of bloodied stones.

The events unfolded on Monday 15 May when Mary informed her uncle, Mr Isbell of Hatherleigh, that she would return from Strawbridge by early evening for dinner and was intending to catch the morning light the following day to finish her landscape. The area in which she set up her easel was one of meadows and grazing cattle, a place where an artist could easily lose track of time. Mr Isbell, however, raised the alarm when Mary failed to return for dinner that evening. He enlisted the help of close friend Mr Veale to search for Mary at her favoured spot and soon found her lifeless body with a bloodied head a short distance from her easel. A doctor was called for and on the pronouncement of death, the body of 'The Artist' was returned to the town where an inquest into her death could begin.

The Dartmoor coroner who presided over the case rushed the inquest and delivered the cause of death as a haemorrhage caused by the horns of charging cattle! Isbell and Veale had noticed, however, that her dress was wet. Reports of the time suggest that the police had not actually checked the location of her death as a crime scene. However, the locals had already decided that this was a case of murder and not one of accidental death.

As rumours intensified, they fed the doubts that Police Sergeant Hill was already feeling about the incident and he instigated his own inquiry into the unusual circumstances of Mary's death. The name that kept popping up was that of John Ware. He had been back in the area for three weeks following his jail term and had found employment ripping bark at nearby Brimridge. The journey to work was a common route but would have taken him past where Mary had been painting and sketching.

John Ware had been lodging at the London Hotel and was noted that evening as returning from work later than usual, having left his work colleagues on the usual way back. He was also noted as appearing nervous, shaking and not making eye contact with people who were talking to him. Although this was circumstantial and not evidence of guilt, people also noticed that the lower half of his trousers was wet. John Ware didn't go to work on the day of Mary's inquest. In fact, he had told colleagues of his desire to leave town and go to Plymouth.

On 17 May John Ware was questioned at Hannahborough Quarry, his new place of work, by Sergeant Hill. The answers weren't forthcoming and so John Ware was removed to Hatherleigh police station and Superintendent Bond from Holsworthy was called for to listen to Ware's defence. It was here that Ware ultimately took his own life. No blame was attached to the police for the death of John Ware. Evidence was, however, found at the crime scene by Bond and Hill. A pile of bloodstained stones close to where the slain body of Mary had been found spoke of past brutality. They were held as murder weapons for the beating and resultant murder of Mary Breton.

Ware's uncoffined, sheeted body was buried on the edge of the graveyard, the truth destined to lie with him for all eternity.

A Chimney Sweep and his Dirty Tricks

ON THE MORNING OF 16 MAY 1854, A FARM WORKER WAS WALKING ALONG THE HEDGEROWED LANES FROM LITTLE TORRINGTON IN DEVON WHEN HE HEARD THE MUTED SOUNDS OF SOMEONE CLOSE TO DEATH. HE PARTED THE THICKET TO GAIN A VIEW INTO THE FIELD WHERE THE UNFORTUNATE VICTIM LAY.

The scene that greeted that labourer's eyes was one he would never forget: twenty-year-old Mary Richards, a local lady, lying in a pool of blood seeping from an open head wound, her clothes about her sullied and dishevelled. Immediately the police were summoned and Mary was taken to a nearby hospital. Although she was close to death, her account of the ordeal she had been put through was lucid. She described her attacker as having gingery facial hair. One name began to surface, based in particular on his public comments about wishing to murder someone, along with his boastful nature and his loathing for the community in which he lived: Llewellyn Garrett Talmage Harvey!

One would be forgiven for thinking that Harvey was from the upper classes, boasting such a name. In fact, he was the son of a lady described as having 'loose morals'. Born in Oxford, his illegitimacy gave him his mother's name of Harvey and his father's name of Talmage. His mother quickly palmed him off on a relative and left the country, and his guardian pushed him into a hand-to-mouth existence as soon as he could. Despite this start in life, Harvey was well educated and tried to better himself from his lowly station, although he concluded that thieving was the only sure way to obtain riches quickly and with minimum effort.

Accused of stealing from houses where he swept chimneys, he was deported to Bermuda, where he served just short of five years of a sentence that was commuted for good behaviour. Harvey returned to England in July 1851 via Quebec and Methodism before he settled down to a disputed marriage and subsequent family in West Putford in September 1852. He was described as a loving husband and a non-drinker who had found religion. By December of that year he had been charged with stealing meat, the ill-gotten gain being found at his house. Most people regarded Harvey as a loathsome failure, which unfortunately for all made him all the more loathsome.

The police remained perplexed, though. Harvey was clean shaven, though everything else fitted the description. Some locals had seen him with hair and others hadn't. Clearly Harvey was changing his appearance to avoid detection in all of his underhand and criminal activities. As a last resort the police decided to bring Harvey to the victim's bedside. She immediately recognised him as the man behind the assault on her. Mary Allen, another local lady, told police that Harvey had tried a similar thing with her only the day before. It transpired that ladies from a nearby glove factory often carried their monies home, having been put into teams of outworkers. On pay day one of the workers would get the team's wages from the factory and pay out her co-workers for the completed goods. Harvey had noted this and had made a list of soft targets in order to pursue his life of petty crime. His rage on Mary was ultimately that of a man thwarted by her changing routines and timings on the home run from the factory.

Is this where Mary Richards meet her end? Goodle Street View

Two weeks later, Mary succumbed to the blows that had been inflicted and now the police were dealing with a murder. Witnesses placed Harvey at the time and location of Mary's fatal encounter with him. Harvey was tried and found guilty of murder after admitting to carrying out the crime. Having hit Mary three times with a hammer, he saw that he had not killed her and, as she tried to crawl to safety, he went back to finish the job. His defence was that he had failed in life, trying to live up to a name that deserved greater standing in society. Harvey wrote his memoirs whilst awaiting execution to earn his family some money after his death. There were no takers.

The Unmarried Mother, the Work-house and the Noose

ON FRIDAY 21 JUNE 1878, A DESPERATE MOTHER OF TWO YOUNG CHILDREN TRAVELLED FROM THE RELATIVE SECURITY OF THE WORKHOUSE AND INTO THE ARMS OF HER BOYFRIEND, JAMES WESTWOOD. THE NEXT DAY, UPON HER RETURN TO THE WORKHOUSE, THE MASTER NOTICED SHE HAD ONLY THE ELDEST OF HER CHILDREN WITH HER.

Selina Wadge was, to all intents and purposes, as much of a victim herself as the soul who ultimately suffered at her hands. Let down by the men in her life, she had not only her own mouth to feed, but those of her offspring. She lived in poverty and by the age of twenty-eight had delivered her two children into a harsh world. We pick up her story when her sons Henry and John are aged two and six. Records describe the younger sibling as having some disability and state that Selina was seen to be doing all she could to feed and care for them. Selina had met a former soldier, James Westwood, and believed they had a strong relationship, hindered only by the encumbrance of her offspring.

50

It appears, though, that much of Selina's understanding of how far the relationship had progressed was wishful thinking on her part, as an ex-soldier was seen to be a 'good catch'. In fact, the couple had met only twice before, the first being six months previous and the last time in March of 1878. Her fateful meeting with James was set and she left the workhouse on Friday 21 June to be in good time for the rendezvous. After hitching a ride to Launceston with a local farmer, she aimed to be back at the workhouse later that evening. However, Selina did not return to the workhouse as promised until midday on Saturday. Witnesses say that they had seen her that morning at Mowbray Park. On her return to the workhouse she was accompanied only by John, her eldest son.

It wasn't long before Selina admitted to her sister, a fellow inmate at the workhouse, as well as to the Workhouse Master that Harry had died at Altarnum. After further questioning on Sunday by the Matron, blame for Harry's disappearance was resting on the shoulders of Selina's boyfriend, James Westwood. Selina told the assembled staff that James had drowned Harry in a well and then threatened to kill both her and John. Immediately, the police were called for and Superintendent Barrett of Launceston police headed up the investigation, ordering an immediate search for the body of the presumed dead child. The small child was eventually found in a covered well, thirteen feet down and in shallow water at Mowbray Park.

Selina remained in the relative safety of the workhouse whil the investigation continued, but later confessed to staff that she had killed her son. She went on to inform police that she had committed the crime because her boyfriend said he would marry her if she did so.

Her trial took place at Bodmin, where testimonials of her good character were presented, but within forty-five minutes a guilty verdict was arrived at and the distasteful event of a woman being hanged was determined. James Westwood did send a letter to Selina as she awaited her death asking for forgiveness. She is reported to have replied verbally to the prison staff that 'he needed forgiveness for many things'.

An appeal for the death penalty to be commuted to one of incarceration in this case was requested, as women found guilty of murdering their children at this time could be reprieved unless the death was through the pre-planned act of poisoning. But it was to no avail. Bodmin Jail was given the spectacle of Selina's punishment, one of four women to be hanged for infanticide in the thirty years from 1869.

Usually for women, discretion was applied to how public the spectacle could be, as hangings were popular and well attended. A board or canvas sheet was sometimes placed over the gates to stop people viewing the event through the various openings. The High Sheriff of Devon forbade the press to witness the execution, which was

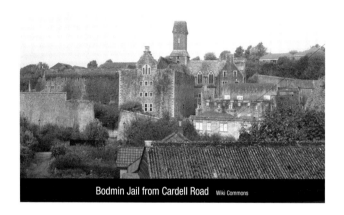

Bodmin Jail from Cardell Road   Wiki Commons

originally scheduled for 12 August but was changed to Thursday 15 August due to the hangman having a prior engagement with an execution elsewhere!

Selina was guarded twenty-four hours a day until the noose was finally placed around her neck. She sobbed on her way to the gallows and her last words were recorded as, 'Lord deliver me from this miserable world.' Handkerchief still in hand, the lever was pulled and her body remained suspended for an hour. Her mortal remains were finally placed to rest within the prison grounds.

Some say her ghost haunts the prison even now. A hand is seen reaching out to small children and the apparition is said to emotionally affect pregnant women. Perhaps a strong emotion such as guilt still spans the years back to that midsummer day in 1878.

Fishing Trip Ends in a Murderous Spree

JAMES HAWKE CAME FROM A TYPICAL TRADES BACKGROUND AND, FROM HIS BIRTHPLACE OF PENZANCE, SOUGHT ADVENTURE THROUGH TRAVEL AFTER UNSUCCESSFULLY TRYING TO JOIN THE NAVY. HE WORKED BRIEFLY AS AN APPRENTICE IN THE TIN TRADE AND IN HIS FORMATIVE YEARS WENT TO SEA ON VARIOUS LOCAL MERCHANT VESSELS.

Penzance Harbour Tom Corser Wiki Commons

James had a good education and was looked up to by fellow students. He showed good academic potential, though it might be seen that social and economic pressures and earning status may have steered his career to more practical and manual labours. He did have a penchant for recording some of his adventures and thoughts in poetic, arguably 'doggerel' pieces, some of which were published in the *Town and Country Journal*.

> *At singing class one day*
>
> *The master said I couldn't sing,*
>
> *But, like an ass, could bray.*
>
> *I laughed at our pedagogue,*
>
> *This happened in Penzance…*
>
> *It's thirty-seven years ago*
>
> *My friends, since this occurred,*
>
> *So out of School I quickly ran…*
>
> *I joined the schooner, Lewis Charles,*
>
> *And went to Wales for coal…*

On returning from his latest excursion from the distant shores of Australia to the familiar territory of his home county, he settled with his sister, Mary Uren, and shoe-smith brother-in-law, Charles Uren, at Marine Place in 1885. Although known to be a drinker and a deserter during his time in Australia, his behaviour was generally well-mannered and his drinking tempered on home shores. Unfortunately, however, the peace was soon to be shattered in a most horrific manner.

Mount's Bay is described as a forty-two-mile stretch of coastline resembling a half moon. Its beauty disguises some of the treachery that the waters there can hide, proving to be dangerous for vessels of all sizes.

At 1.30 pm on 28 July, 1886, James Hawke, known locally as 'Old Bird' from both his name and his ornithological interests, returned from fishing at the bay along with a few of his acquaintances. One could imagine the mood being light, with the usual banter about the ones that got away, but soon this was to turn like the tides he had so often ridden upon. Within a few minutes of returning to the comfort of his sister's family home, the fifty-one-year-old became possessed of murderous intent. Raised voices were heard. Neighbour John Searle, a mariner himself, had seen the men leave earlier in the day, but soon upon their return heard gunshots that must have torn through the silence like a cannon going off. Three people lay dead.

It seems that James Hawke had returned with the drink in him, something Mary had seen before and questioned him about. The inquest reports that Hawke, 'in a passion', shouted, *'If you b......s don't clear out from here, I'll be damned to soon settle the lot of you!' Mr Gerard, the local jeweller, and his wife had been visiting the Urens and thought it best to leave as tempers were flaring. As they left, two gunshots rang out and Mrs Gerard ran back, saying to Hawke, 'I have not said anything to you, Mr Hawke, have I?'*

Hawke raised the pistol and fired two bullets into Mrs Gerard, prompting Mr Gerard to run to her side asking if she was dead. At this moment, Mr Searle saw Hawke pass a small bag to another neighbour, Mrs Roberts, saying to deliver this to Clara, his niece. Upon this transaction, Hawke raised the gun a final time, this time to his head, and pulled the trigger. Searle ran to Hawke and moved the gun away from his hand before calling for the police.

The inquest into the horrors that followed this fishing trip described the crimes as 'circumstances of exceptional horror, the surroundings of the case being shocking and appalling'. The outcome of the inquest reported that the actions of Hawke had been deliberate and not made through the haze of drink, as Hawke had needed to reload his weapon. It was done in a 'cool' and 'calm' manner.

The verdict was murder and suicide. The news of this multiple murder spread around the world. The reasons for the change in Hawke's temperament were discussed and, although not conclusive, were linked unreliably to changes in his manner while in Australia. The *Town and Country Journal* made a brief report on the killings with no connection being made to the man or his contributions to the publication.

Hawke, it seems, remains an enigma. He was described as penniless and had not worked since his return from Australia. It might be argued that he returned to home shores with his spirit broken and his mind ready to become unhinged at the merest hint of perceived criticisms.

The Young Sibling, the Word and a Silk Handkerchief

DELIVERANCE FROM THIS WORLD TO THE NEXT IS TRAUMATIC ENOUGH WITHOUT IT BEING AT THE HANDS OF ANOTHER. EVEN GREATER CONFUSION IS CAUSED WHEN THE CRIME IS COMMITTED BY A LOVED ONE INDOCTRINATED BY A SKEWED APPLICATION OF FAITH, A SUSCEPTIBLE MIND AND RELIGIOUS AMBIGUITY.

Launceston David P Howard CC

Nineteen-year-old Amy George lived with her parents in Redruth and in March 1824 made the decision to end her younger brother's life. Amy appears to have been misguided by the rites of a cult and its religious indoctrination. As ever, the importance of understanding the implications of something before it is fully understood and then passing on that limited knowledge to an impressionable mind is fraught with danger, never more so than in this sad tale of misguided and misrepresented faith.

At this time reports in the *Newgate Calendar* tell us that 'Revival' meetings were being held up and down the country, but the cultish nature of some other more delusional orders were also spreading their word through the infiltration of Methodist gatherings. During the ritual, ecstatic fervour often boiled over through the 'outpouring of the spirit' and 'screeching for mercy', deemed cleansing until Benediction and the 'point of conversion' resulting in the vision of 'the ray of hope'. In some factions this concept was misused and debased in an attempt to increase the flock. It was believed that divine favour would be bestowed upon the order by releasing the souls of children below the age of seven years, before they had gained an age of perceived 'free will'. This abomination was brought into sharp focus on 4 March 1824.

Amy worked at the nearby mine and had been attending religious meetings for some time, but had recently developed a strong and irrational urge to murder her mother and indeed had prayed to God that she wouldn't carry it through. However, at the mine several opportunities presented themselves to slake her thirst for murder by simply pushing the children who worked there into a pit-head grave. Some of these children had nothing but drudgery in their lives and therefore wouldn't be 'missed'. Again, Amy fought with her conscience until that fateful March day when she was left for the evening to take care of her young brother, Benny. The children's mother went to another meeting of the faith and as she left the house she told Amy that her supper was ready and to eat it while she was out.

After eating her supper, Amy asked Benny if he would like to go to heaven. Walking over to a line of washing, she took a black silk handkerchief and knotted it around Benny's neck, checking with him that it wasn't too tight. She then asked if he would fetch some water from a nearby pail, as she was thirsty after the repast. Drinking from the cup her brother had obediently placed in her hand, she lifted him up and hung him by the handkerchief she had placed about his neck from a crook behind a door. Looking him in the eye and leaving him to die, she left the room for the time that would be needed to take the innocent to heaven.

On Amy's arrest, Mrs George spoke of the increasingly deranged nature of her daughter following these questionable gatherings. At one such outpouring, Amy let several items of her clothing slip to the floor and, losing them to the ecstatic crowd, she noticed her mother and, raising her arms, called both parents to pray with her as they didn't know the danger they were in. After one meeting, Amy disclosed to her mother that she thought she was losing her mind and that she felt predisposed to kill someone. When her mother asked whether Amy wanted to kill her, she replied in the affirmative. Disturbed by this, Mrs George removed all things from reach that she considered dangerous and that potentially could do the family harm. Unfortunately for Benny, a black silk handkerchief was not seen to be a danger.

At Launceston Assizes on 1 April the sad and disturbing story of Benny's death unfolded and, at its conclusion, Amy fainted and went into convulsions, screaming wildly for some fifteen minutes. The jury returned a verdict of not guilty of murder, as they deemed the girl insane at the time of assault. She was held in custody until such time as she would no longer be a danger to herself or those around her.

Whether Amy's state of mind was altered by religious zeal and fervour or its persuasive nature only added further disruption to an already disturbed mind is left open to discussion. Was she so susceptible that she would act directly on the words that were uttered by this perverted splinter of faith? Should its parasitical nature in using a mainstream faith to convey its warped message have been allowed? One will never know what went through the eyes and minds of Amy and Benny on that tragic day in Redruth.

Highway Murder

THE LANES AND TRADE ROUTES ALONG ANCIENT ROADS AND BYWAYS WERE ALWAYS DANGEROUS, BUT ESPECIALLY SO AT THE END OF A BUSINESS DAY WHEN LIGHT WAS FADING FROM THE SKY AND THE SHADOWY FORCES OF MALCONTENTS MOVED IN. HIGHWAY ROBBERY THAT INVOLVED SIMPLY THE LIFTING OF A FULL PURSE WAS ALWAYS A RISK, BUT SOMETIMES A SIMPLE ROBBERY TURNED TO MURDER.

Helston, along with Redruth, has always been a busy commercial town. In the nineteenth century, the region around St Ives and Camborne helped Cornwall provide more than two thirds of the global output in copper production. Together with arable farming, fishing and brick making, this diversity of industries created potential for great wealth and, in so doing, provided rich and easy pickings from the wealth that was transiting the main routes between towns.

An engine house near Helston
Chris Allen CC

The evening of 12 August 1820 was a particularly busy one and saw many a robbery along one such highway near to Helston. One of these attacks left one man mortally wounded and, in another case, a couple recovering from the viciousness of the attack on them.

William Hancock was the unfortunate traveller that evening. He not only lost his money but was to pay the ultimate cost of his life. He was shot and beaten up so badly that he died after a few days of clinging on to this world. Every so often, though, a murder case relies on the last person to see the perpetrator and William did just this. Before he died, chief suspect John Barnicoat (sometimes spelled Barnicot) was bought before the dying William Hancock where he quickly identified the man as one of the three assailants. William Hancock faced remonstrations of innocence from Barnicoat, but he asked of his attacker how he could say what he said after he had threatened him with a long wooden staff, saying that he would knock his brains out. Thought to be accompanying Barnicoat were the brothers John and Thomas Thompson.

All three men were placed into custody and awaited their trial at the March sessions. As this declaration from William Hancock had been his dying statement, great weight was placed upon it as being a true and representative account of the events of that evening. The trial took place on 30 March 1821. Without William

Hancock being available for cross-questioning, the statement of truth and the burden of guilt were pretty much unassailable by the defence.

John Barnicoat produced witness statements to say that he wasn't on that stretch of road that evening and, therefore, could not be guilty of William's murder. However, certain aspects of the alibis contradicted each other and were, therefore, discredited. Thomas Thompson did walk from court an innocent man in the eyes of the jury, as William Hancock had not formally accused him of anything, and so it was just John Barnicoat and the seventeen-year-old John Thompson who faced their sentence and a walk to the gallows. These were situated on a small mound on Launceston Castle Green not far from the ruins of the old castle and the remains of what is known locally as the Witch's Tower. The nearby Exeter Inn provided shelter for some of the relatives awaiting the body of their nearest to be cut down from the gibbet, but it is not known whether these branded murderers had anyone wait for them on 2 April 1821 at 9.30 am.

John Barnicoat appeared to take his fate in his stride and accepted his execution as he was escorted to the waiting rope. John Thompson, however, found the last walk too much and needed to sit down to support his collapsing frame. As the chaplain asked the men for the final time to admit their guilt, John Barnicoat maintained his innocence, saying he knew nothing of the murder or any other attacks on that August evening and held firm that he had been *abed* on the said evening. He called to John Thompson to qualify his statement of innocence. John Thompson concurred, saying it had been him and his brother and the murderous Thomas Dawe who had carried out the attacks, and that Dawe was the man who shot William Hancock. John Thompson admitted that it was he who had threatened Mr Hancock with a pike handle while Mr Hancock was on the ground with a gunshot wound.

As the chaplain said prayers for the two accused, a large crowd had gathered to see the spectacle before them. It was John Barnicoat who first signalled that he was ready to face all eternity. The lever was pulled on both men who swung, whether guilty or not guilty, their destinies claimed by the word of a dead man.

Last in Line at Bodmin

THE LAST IN A LONG LINE OF CONVICTS AT THE NOOSE END OF A BODMIN ROPE FINALLY APPEARED ON 20 JULY 1909: A YOUNG MURDERER, WILLIAM HAMPTON, WHO HAD STRANGLED HIS LOVER.

William Hampton had returned home in 1907 from several years of working in America. Hampton was around twenty-one years of age when he met his then fifteen-year-old girlfriend, Emily Barnes Trevarthen Tredea. Hampton had only recently moved from his nearby mother's house to live with his girlfriend at her mother's home. The house had three young children in it, as well as Emily and her mother. A fair assumption can be made that it must have been a crowded environment with little personal space.

On 2 May 1909 in this house on Village Row, St Erth, a nine-year-old boy heard strange sounds coming from downstairs in his home. His mother was out tending to a sick neighbour and he therefore wanted to know what was happening in his house. Out of a sense of duty to his younger siblings, he took responsibility and,

St Erth Bill Boaden CC

bravely, as the 'man of the house', went downstairs to see what the trouble was. When he got there, he saw twenty-three-year-old William Hampton kneeling on the chest of his seventeen-year-old sister, his bare hands strangling the last breaths of life from her limp body. Her pale complexion was now blue with asphyxia and her lips were badly swollen. During the attack, Emily's brother shouted to Hampton to 'Get back!' Hampton, in a state of ferment, took no notice of him and continued with what he had started.

Emily's brother ran upstairs that night and got dressed before returning to his sister and Hampton. Emily's body had been pushed so hard in the attack that her head was now against a door. The boy was helpless to do anything to aid his sister and must have feared that she was, in fact, beyond help.

Earlier that evening, Emily had been out with friends and returned to her home at around 10 o'clock. Her mother handed her the baby of the house, saying that she was needed to tend to Hampton's sick mother, and left the house. It was around this time that the couple began to argue and Emily was heard to say that she didn't want to go out with Hampton any more.

After the assault, Emily's brother saw Hampton sit the lifeless body of his sister in a chair. She promptly slid to the floor, and so Hampton tried sitting her in an armchair made of wicker that finally did support Emily's lifeless body. In fear and dread, Emily's brother ran to find his mother and tell her of the horrors he had witnessed that evening. Hampton ran off shortly afterwards, only to give himself up to the police a few hours later, admitting it was he who had 'choked the girl'.

When poor Emily's body was found, she was certified dead. A plate of cake on a nearby table was considered a potential cause of choking, but none was found in her mouth. In fact, she had been starved of air for three to four minutes through strangulation and all the evidence rested on her brother's witness testimony.

At the trial, it was debated whether Hampton had only meant to teach Emily a lesson and that the intention was not to kill her. In fact, a crime of passion plea could have been drawn upon and, to some degree, discussed as a motive. It seems that Hampton's rage was based on Emily going out with her friends, rather than walking out with him. It also seems likely that Emily then decided to break off her engagement to Hampton as a result of the ensuing argument. However, one report says that the strangulation did not follow on immediately after this argument and that they had appeared 'friendly' afterwards. If this is so, it clearly indicates an argument revisited or that Hampton had committed murder in cold blood. Had it been deemed to be in the heat of the moment, Hampton may have got away with a manslaughter charge.

Hampton was sentenced to death for the murder of Emily, but he also received a recommendation of reprieve based on circumstances surrounding the murder, in that he had been previously noted as a good and honest man and that the murder was not premeditated, as no weapon had been obtained to be used upon the girl. It was also regarded that the evidence from Emily's nine-year-old brother be taken with caution because of his age. But no reviews were made of this case and the evidence held firm.

William Hampton was the last man to be hanged at Bodmin Jail and, indeed, the last one in Cornwall. The execution took place on 20 July 1909, the man who pulled the lever being none other than Henry Pierrepoint, from the well-known family of executioners and father of the famous Albert. (Henry's career was cut short, however, when he turned up drunk for an execution in 1910. In his eight and a half years or so as executioner, he recorded 105 executions and his diaries contained physical descriptions of the guilty so that he always got the weight and the height of the drop right.)

Hampton's body was then removed to an unmarked grave within the prison grounds, though someone did carve and place a stone with the initials WH upon it. Emily's grave carried no headstone and the simple plot marker that identified her has long since perished, but a memorial stone was placed there by relatives in 2011.

Oh, Between Two and Five Pounds

CHARLOTTE WINSOR OF TORQUAY APPEARED TO BE YOUR AVERAGE VICTORIAN NEIGHBOUR. BUT HER LIFE WAS FAR FROM ORDINARY. THE NEWS OF HER CONTRACTED SERIAL KILLINGS OF CHILDREN HAD BECOME WIDELY KNOWN IN 1865. CHISEL FACED, HAIR SCRAPED BACK, CONSERVATIVELY DRESSED AND WEARING A BONNET TIED WITH A BOW UNDER HER CHIN, SHE AWAITED JUDGEMENT.

The *Illustrated Police News* pamphlet produced between 1866 and 1867 was already being reprinted, such were its sales. Described as 'sixteen handsome pages' by the publishers, it sold for a penny plus a penny postage to those wanting to read the true horrors of the life of a serial killer. It contained details of the trial and even showed a sketch of the cottage where the murders took place! The advertising for the publication was as follows:

'Full particulars of her life from authentic sources. The supposed number of her Victims. Mary Harris turning Queen's Evidence. Her Three Husbands. Full account of her Low and Dissolute Habits. Fearful Revelations of Infanticide in England.'

Charlottle Winsor

Included in this souvenir pamphlet was a portrait of how Charlotte Winsor appeared in the dock! The above sounds more like the headline grabbers of a modern-day tawdry tabloid or online clickbait than a police journal.

Twice in 1865 'baby farmer' (a term used for a person paid to take in children) Charlotte Winsor, who was forty-five years of age, and twenty-three year old Mary Jane Harris appeared before the court of Exeter's Devon Assizes.

On a bitterly cold February day near to the town of Torquay, a small bundle wrapped in newspaper and tied with a high-quality wool yarn known as 'worsted' was found on a nearby road. Within the bundle lay the body of Thomas Edward Gibson Harris, an infant child of an estimated four months of age. Due to the weather conditions, it was deemed that it was either exposure that had killed the child or suffocation. The question remained, however, as to who had placed the child there and why.

Police investigated recent birth records and gradually built up a list of suspects for questioning, which ultimately led to the mother being identified as Mary Harris, a servant living with Charlotte Winsor, Charlotte's husband and her grandchild. Mary's child was known to be illegitimate.

Mr Baron Channell presided over the evidence of this tragically short life and the findings of the court led to the jury being dismissed, as no clear verdict could be reached. There seemed nothing else for it than to get a fair outcome. Mr Baron Channell agreed to let Mary speak by turning Queen's evidence. For those not in the know, 'turning Queen's evidence' is a legal term for someone who is jointly charged with a crime choosing to give additional evidence to a trial against the co-accused in the hope of gaining some leniency in their own sentence.

The story of poor Thomas's short life came to the ears of the courtroom from Mary's statement. She had been working as a servant for a Mrs Wansey, but had recently given birth to a male child, one it appears she couldn't afford to keep. Harris had met Winsor about six months before and knew of her practices. Winsor had made no secret of how she easily dispatched 'unwanted infants'. The meeting at Marychurch the previous September had offered Mary a way out of her predicament. Winsor had boasted to her of previous services to other mothers. These included another girl who had gone to Winsor's cottage for her confinement and then had 'sold' her child's life for a fee of three pounds to Winsor, only for the payment to be unforthcoming. The three-week-old child of Elizabeth Sharland, another client, had been thrown into the sea at Torbay and when the body was found it was so badly decomposed that it was beyond recognition. Elizabeth's sister's child was put up for four pounds after a letter was left for the child's father at the Jolly Sailor pub, the father being a sailor who left the money, but she only gave Winsor two pounds of that.

Thus the stories of these dark deeds continued, revealing the full extent of Winsor's callous nature as it became courtroom fact. Harris made her way from Mrs Wansey's Tamar Villas address to that of the Winsors' Shiphay Bridge cottage. Harris had asked Winsor how she 'did it'. Winsor explained that she placed a finger upon the jugular and applied pressure. The ensuing conversations between the two ladies revealed that Winsor believed she was doing good and that she would 'help' anyone who stayed quiet about what she was doing. The visit lasted half an hour. They even had tea before the deed was performed. As Harris left the house, Winsor calmly reassured Harris that she would do 'whatever lays in my powers for your child'. The decision was made then to put an end to the infant's life for the sum of five pounds. Winsor asked Harris to put the child 'between the bedticks' (bags that contain bed linen). Winsor took the child into her granddaughter's room and murdered Thomas by smothering him. Winsor at this time still believed she was 'doing good'.

As Harris told her story, the stoic stance of Winsor began to show cracks in its calm exterior, which led to a couple of hours of hysteria and tears. Within an hour, the jury delivered the verdict of guilty to the court. Charlotte Winsor was to be hanged and she should not hope for any mercy upon the decision. However, despite her grave being dug and having been visited twice by the executioner, Winsor's sentence was ultimately commuted to life imprisonment and Harris was absolved of any charge due to her evidence. Twenty-two years later, the *St James Gazette* commented upon the fact that, despite being guilty of such heinous crimes, Charlotte Winsor was at that time still living.

Two Sisters, Two Stories – Madness or Love?

THE STORY OF TWO SISTERS AND THEIR SIBLING RIVALRY TAKES US BACK IN TIME AND PLACE TO A FIFTEENTH-CENTURY CASTLE. DEVON'S BERRY POMEROY CASTLE IS REPUTED TO BE ONE OF THE MOST HAUNTED PLACES IN BRITAIN, BUT JUST WHAT IS THE STORY OF THE 'WHITE LADY' WHO IS STILL BEWAILING HER UNJUST INCARCERATION ACROSS THE CENTURIES?

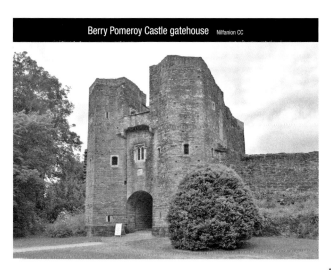

Berry Pomeroy Castle gatehouse   Nilfanion CC

Berry Pomeroy Castle lies in the rich landscape of South Devon not far from Torquay and Paignton. The Pomeroy family owned the lands for around four hundred years before building the castle in the late 1400s. Unfortunately for the family, finances ran short and in 1547, after the property and land had become forfeit to the crown, it was sold to Edward Seymour.

There are many stories about this powerful Devon family and its rise and fall in dignity and respect prior to the sale. That is for other publications to explore and for you, dear reader, to research if you wish! But for those who want a historical rewind and fast forward in time, here we go!

There are stories of brothers riding blindfolded horses over the ramparts to their deaths when under Edward VI's siege due to religious rebellion. Of a Norman Lord father's reputed incestuous relationship with his daughter that led to infanticide. Of a sixteenth-century manor extension and its use as a place of execution when in the hands of the Crown before being struck by lightning. This is followed by seventeenth-century abandonment and subsequently falling into ruin.

As the centuries blur memories and stories become generational whispers that flex and distort in the winds of time, facts are difficult to pull together. However, this particular story takes us to a favourite landmark in Devon at a time in the fifteenth century when the Crusades were still thought to be a just and noble cause and many men went and fought for their faith in lands far from these shores. This often meant many years abroad and, if they ever returned home, they were often much changed through experience. One father, Henry Pomeroy, left his daughters behind to fight such a battle. His story is overshadowed to some degree by the pristine white figure, described by thousands over the years, that rises above St Margaret's Tower, believed to be the apparition of Henry's murdered daughter, Lady Margaret.

Ladies Margaret and Eleanor would have had a high standard of living for their times and enjoyed many fine things in life, but their world would have been suffocatingly small and potential suitors difficult to engage with. One story of the sisters' paths crossing in a romantic outpouring sees the two of them falling in love with the same young man. Lady Eleanor was put in charge of the castle whilst her father was away, but it wasn't long before her jealousy, assumed to be the greater of the two, felt the need to remove any opposition to the young man's attentions. She therefore decided that Margaret should 'disappear' for a while. This she achieved by luring Margaret into the dungeons set deep in the castle and effectively throwing away the key. Margaret's death would have been a painful one, rumoured to span twenty years of neglect, a slow and lingering demise, eventually of starvation, as Eleanor entertained her young man.

A second story of the two sisters is that Eleanor had placed Margaret into the dungeons to keep her safe from herself and from harming others. The story goes that Margaret was suffering from a form of madness and was therefore locked away because of it. Many stigmas were associated with mental health conditions and so signs of weakness or 'feeblemindedness' may have led to the locking away of Margaret. Whatever the reason, and whether madness preceded love or love created madness, we may never know, but Margaret would have died a sad and lonely death at the distant and uncaring hands of her sister.

When Henry returned from the Crusades, he placed responsibility for Margaret's death firmly on Eleanor's shoulders and held her accountable for the loss of his younger daughter. And so we come back to two sisters at war. Was it love or madness? Who are the restless spirits? Who is the lady in white: an aggrieved Margaret or a guilty Eleanor? Whatever the story, it remains an injustice that echoes through the centuries and may never be resolved.

As a footnote, in *The Castle of Berry Pomeroy* Edward Montague weaves fact with fiction in this 1806 Gothic novel.